Meet Jesus

The Life and Lessons of a Beloved Teacher

WRITTEN BY LYNN TUTTLE GUNNEY

ILLUSTRATED BY JANE CONTEH-MORGAN

Printed in the United States.

Illustrations by Jane Conteh-Morgan
Text and cover design by Suzanne Morgan

ISBN 1-55896-524-6
978-1-55896-524-9

5 4 3 2 1
10 09 08 07

Library of Congress Cataloging-in-Publication Data

Gunney, Lynn Tuttle.
  Meet Jesus : the life and lessons of a beloved teacher / Lynn Tuttle Gunney.
      p. cm.
   ISBN-13: 978-1-55896-524-9 (pbk. : alk. paper)
   ISBN-10: 1-55896-524-6 (pbk. : alk. paper) 1. Jesus Christ—Juvenile literature. I. Title.
BT302.G86 2007
232.9—dc22
                              2007004747

The Bible passages in this book are from the World English Bible, an online translation based on the American Standard Version of 1901. Although this translation contains some sexist language, we are using it because it is in the public domain. The full translation is available online at www.ebible.org. The World English Bible is still considered a draft, but no major changes are expected in the final version of the New Testament.

For Annam and Trian—
To know your mother's spiritual roots

This is the story of Jesus, a beloved teacher. Although he lived long ago, his lessons of love and kindness still bring hope and joy to people all over the world.

Jesus was born more than two thousand years ago in a land now called Israel. He grew up in the town of Nazareth with his brothers and sisters and their parents, Mary and Joseph.

Luke 2:4–6, 39–40

Joseph was a carpenter. He taught Jesus how to shape rough wooden logs into sturdy beams for building homes. He showed Jesus how to make plows and shovels that were straight and strong. And he helped Jesus craft tables and chairs and cups and bowls that were both beautiful and useful.

Joseph and Mary raised Jesus in the traditions of their Jewish faith. Jesus learned to read the Torah, a sacred book that Jewish people believe was inspired by God. As Jesus and Joseph worked side by side in the carpentry shop, they talked about religion. Jesus felt a strong connection to God. He began to sense that God had called him to bring people a new message of love and forgiveness.

John 14:6–7

Every year, Jesus' family celebrated the Jewish
holiday of Passover in the city of Jerusalem, the center
of Jewish life. Jesus loved to sit among the teachers at
the great temple, listening to their lively conversations.
He was very curious and asked many questions. The
teachers were amazed at how much he understood.

When he grew up, Jesus began to travel the
countryside and tell people his ideas about living
together in peace and harmony. Soon crowds gathered
to hear him preach. People who were sick often came
to him, and he helped them feel better. News of Jesus
as a healer and teacher spread.

Matthew 4:23–25

Jesus did not do this work alone. A group of men and women traveled with him. He chose twelve friends, called disciples, to help him teach his ideas to others. "Come, follow me," he said to the disciples. Together they walked from village to village, sharing their new ideas with anyone who wanted to listen.

Luke 8:1–3; Mark 3:13–14

Jesus said we should love one another because God loves us. God loves each one of us, even when we make mistakes or do wrong. This idea of God surprised people.

Jesus often told stories, or parables, to teach people about God. One day he told this parable: "Once there was a shepherd who looked after a flock of one hundred sheep. When the shepherd noticed that one little lamb was missing, he was very upset. Leaving the flock, the shepherd searched high and low from dawn to dusk. When he finally found the lost lamb, he was filled with joy."

This parable helped Jesus explain how God loves and cares for each one of us, just like the shepherd loves and cares for each one of his sheep.

Luke 6:35–36; Matthew 18:12–14

Mothers and fathers brought their sons and daughters to meet Jesus. At first, the disciples waved them away, worried that the children would bother Jesus. But Jesus gathered the children around him and blessed them. "Let the little children come to me," he said.

Mark 10:13–16

Jesus believed we should love one another, even people who aren't our friends. "Treat everyone the way you would like them to treat you," he taught. "Love your neighbor as much as you love yourself." Someone asked, "But who is my neighbor?" Jesus answered with another parable.

John 13:34; Luke 6:27–28; Matthew 7:12, 22:39

Once upon a time there was a Jewish man who was attacked by robbers while on a journey from Jerusalem to Jericho. A traveler walked by and saw the man lying injured by the side of the road, but didn't even stop to help. Another traveler came along but did not stop either.

Then a Samaritan walked by. The Samaritan could see that the injured man was a Jew. Even though Samaritans and Jews had different religious beliefs and often did not get along, this traveler stopped to help. The Samaritan cleaned and bandaged the injured man's wounds, then helped him onto his donkey, took him to an inn, and paid for his stay until the man was well enough to travel again.

As the crowd listened, Jesus told them, "Go and care for one another like the good Samaritan did." We are all neighbors. We can show our love for others by taking care of all people who need help.

13

Jesus taught his followers to look for ways to live together in harmony, to learn to forgive, and to settle arguments in a peaceful way. "Blessed are those who work to bring peace to the world," he said, "for they are children of God."

Matthew 5:9, 23–24, 38–39

One of the disciples asked, "What if someone treats me badly? How many times should I forgive—seven times?" Jesus answered, "No, not seven times, but seventy times seven times!" Jesus meant that we should always forgive one another, just as God forgives us.

Matthew 18:21–22, 6:14

As he went from village to village, Jesus reached out to help sick people get well and to feed those who were hungry. He treated everyone with the same kindness— women and men, Jews and non-Jews, rich and poor, good and bad.

Matthew 9:35, 15:32–38; John 4:7–10; Luke 19:1–7; Mark 2:15–17

By now Jesus had many followers, but not everyone was happy about it. The leaders in Jerusalem noticed the big crowds that gathered whenever Jesus spoke. They wondered if the people might quit turning to them for advice, and stop following their rules and traditions.

Once the disciples knew that the leaders disapproved of Jesus, they were worried. When they gathered for their Passover meal that year, Jesus blessed the bread and wine and gave thanks to God. "May peace be with you," he said to the disciples. Jesus asked them to remember him and his lessons, no matter what happened.

Today this meal is known as the Last Supper. Some people share bread and wine in church as a way to remember it.

Luke 22:8, 14, 17, 19–20; John 14:27

After the Last Supper, things happened fast. Soldiers arrested Jesus, saying that he was stirring up trouble. In those days, the worst criminals were punished by being nailed to a wooden cross and left to die. Jesus was punished in this terrible way.

Mark 14:43, 46; Mark 15:16–20

As Jesus suffered on the cross, his mother, Mary, and his friends gathered at his side. They knew Jesus had done nothing wrong. They were filled with sadness.

After Jesus died, his followers carried on his teaching and honored his memory. Jesus' message of love and kindness spread throughout the world.

Now, two thousand years later, we can still learn from the life and lessons of Jesus. Some people say that Jesus was the son of God. They say that after Jesus died, God resurrected him, or brought him back to life. They celebrate his resurrection on Easter Sunday. Some people say that Jesus was a wise and beloved teacher, whether or not he was the son of God. They say it is important to remember him because he taught us to treat people with love and to stand up for justice and peace.

No one knows for sure what day Jesus was born, but many people celebrate his birthday on Christmas Day, December 25. This is a day of joy and generosity spent with family and friends, sharing food, singing songs, and giving gifts.

We celebrate the life of Jesus by trying to live as he did, with full hearts, loving words, and kind actions.

Questions to Think About

- What good deeds have you done for others?

- When have you forgiven someone? What did it feel like?

- Has anyone ever forgiven you for something? What did that feel like?

- Have you heard your friends or grown-ups talking about Jesus? What did they say?

- Why do some people need to be reminded to be kind?

- Is it hard to be nice to someone who is mean to you? Why?

Dear Parents and Teachers,

Children are naturals at drawing lessons from stories. The story of Jesus was not written down until a generation after his death. Before then it was kept alive as an oral tradition. We have no texts from Jesus himself, only others' accounts of his life and teachings. The best-known of these are collected and preserved in the Bible.

In this book, I introduce Jesus as a beloved teacher rather than as a divine figure. My telling of Jesus' story is based on a liberal religious interpretation of the Bible. I recognize that others have different perspectives, and I encourage you to discuss your own understanding with the children in your lives. To help you do that, I include in the following pages the Bible passages that I used as sources and inspiration for this book.

Jesus offers a model of love and compassion that has inspired and comforted people for generations. May it be so for you and yours.

Lynn T. Gunney
Lynn Tuttle Gunney

Bible Passages

Luke 2:4–6, 39–40

Joseph also went up from Galilee, out of the city of Nazareth, into Judea, to the city of David, which is called Bethlehem, because he was of the house and family of David; to enroll himself with Mary, who was pledged to be married to him as wife, being pregnant. It happened, while they were there, that the day had come that she should give birth. . . . When they had accomplished all things that were according to the law of the Lord, they returned into Galilee, to their own city, Nazareth. The child was growing, and was becoming strong in spirit, being filled with wisdom, and the grace of God was upon him.

Matthew 13:55

Isn't this the carpenter's son? Isn't his mother called Mary, and his brothers, James, Joses, Simon, and Judas?

John 14:6–7

Jesus said to him, "I am the way, the truth, and the life. No one comes to the Father, except through me. If you had known me, you would have known my Father also. From now on, you know him, and have seen him."

Luke 2:46–47

It happened after three days they found him in the temple, sitting in the midst of the teachers, both listening to them, and asking them questions. All who heard him were amazed at his understanding and his answers.

Matthew 4:23–25

Jesus went about in all Galilee, teaching in their synagogues, preaching the Good News of the Kingdom, and healing every disease and every sickness among the people. The report about him went out into all Syria. They brought to him all who were sick, afflicted with various diseases and torments, possessed with demons, epileptics, and paralytics; and he healed them. Great multitudes from Galilee, Decapolis, Jerusalem, Judea and from beyond the Jordan followed him.

Luke 8:1–3

It happened soon afterwards, that he went about through cities and villages, preaching and bringing the good news of the Kingdom of God. With him were the twelve, and certain women who had been healed of evil spirits and infirmities: Mary who was called Magdalene, from whom seven demons had gone out; and Joanna, the wife of Chuzas, Herod's steward; Susanna; and many others; who served them from their possessions.

Mark 3:13–14

He went up into the mountain, and called to himself those whom he wanted, and they went to him. He appointed twelve, that they might be with him, and that he might send them out to preach. . . .

Luke 6:35–36

But love your enemies, and do good, and lend, expecting nothing back; and your reward will be great, and you will be children of the Most High; for he is kind toward the unthankful and evil. Therefore be merciful, even as your Father is also merciful.

Matthew 18:12–14

If a man has one hundred sheep, and one of them goes astray, doesn't he leave the ninety-nine, go to the mountains, and seek that which has gone astray? If he finds it, most certainly I tell you, he rejoices over it more than over the ninety-nine which have not gone astray. Even so it is not the will of your Father who is in heaven that one of these little ones should perish.

John 13:34

A new commandment I give to you, that you love one another, just like I have loved you; that you also love one another.

Luke 6:27–28

Love your enemies, do good to those who hate you, bless those who curse you, and pray for those who mistreat you.

Matthew 7:12

Therefore whatever you desire for men to do to you, you shall also do to them; for this is the law and the prophets.

Matthew 22:39

A second likewise is this, "You shall love your neighbor as yourself."

Luke 10:29–37

But he, desiring to justify himself, asked Jesus, "Who is my neighbor?" Jesus answered, "A certain man was going down from Jerusalem to Jericho, and he fell among robbers, who both stripped him and beat him, and departed, leaving him half dead. By chance a certain priest was going down that way. When he saw him, he passed by on the other side. In the same way a Levite also, when he came to the place, and saw him, passed by on the other side. But a certain Samaritan, as he traveled, came where he was. When he saw him, he was moved with compassion, came to him, and bound up his wounds, pouring on oil and wine. He set him on his own animal, and brought him to an inn, and took care of him. On the next day, when he departed, he took out two denarii, and gave them to the host, and said to him, 'Take care of him. Whatever you spend beyond that, I will repay you when I return.' Now which of these three do you think seemed to be a neighbor to him who fell among the robbers?" He said,

"He who showed mercy on him." Then Jesus said to him, "Go and do likewise."

Mark 10:13–16

They were bringing to him little children, that he should touch them, but the disciples rebuked those who were bringing them. But when Jesus saw it, he was moved with indignation, and said to them, "Allow the little children to come to me! Don't forbid them, for the Kingdom of God belongs to such as these. Most certainly I tell you, whoever will not receive the Kingdom of God like a little child, he will in no way enter into it." He took them in his arms, and blessed them, laying his hands on them.

Matthew 5:9

Blessed are the peacemakers, for they shall be called children of God.

Matthew 5:23–24

If therefore you are offering your gift at the altar, and there remember that your brother has anything against you, leave your gift there before the altar, and go your way. First be reconciled to your brother, and then come and offer your gift.

Matthew 5:38–39

You have heard that it was said, "An eye for an eye, and a tooth for a tooth." But I tell you, don't resist him who is evil; but whoever strikes you on your right cheek, turn to him the other also.

Matthew 18:21–22

Then Peter came and said to him, "Lord, how often shall my brother sin against me, and I forgive him? Until seven times?" Jesus said to him, "I don't tell you until seven times, but, until seventy times seven."

Matthew 6:14

For if you forgive men their trespasses, your heavenly Father will also forgive you. But if you don't forgive men their trespasses, neither will your Father forgive your trespasses.

Matthew 9:35

Jesus went about all the cities and the villages, teaching in their synagogues, and preaching the Good News of the Kingdom, and healing every disease and every sickness among the people.

Matthew 15:32–38

Jesus summoned his disciples and said, "I have compassion on the multitude, because they continue with me now three days and have nothing to eat. I don't want to send them away fasting, or they might faint on the way." The disciples said to him, "Where should we get so many loaves in a deserted place as to satisfy so great a multitude?" Jesus said to them, "How many loaves do you have?" They said, "Seven, and a few small fish." He commanded the multitude to sit down on the ground; and he took the seven loaves and the fish. He gave thanks and broke them, and gave to the disciples, and the disciples to the multitudes. They all ate, and were filled. They took up seven baskets full of the broken pieces that were left over. Those who ate were four thousand men, besides women and children.

John 4:7–10

A woman of Samaria came to draw water. Jesus said to her, "Give me a drink." For his disciples had gone away into the city to buy food. The Samaritan woman therefore said to him, "How is it that you, being a Jew, ask for a drink from me, a Samaritan woman?" (For Jews have no dealings with Samaritans.) Jesus answered her, "If you knew the gift of God, and who it is who says to you, 'Give me a drink,' you would have asked him, and he would have given you living water."

Luke 19:1–7

He entered and was passing through Jericho. There was a man named Zacchaeus. He was a chief tax collector, and he was rich. He was trying to see who Jesus was, and couldn't because of the crowd, because he was short. He ran on ahead, and climbed up into a sycamore tree to see him, for he was to pass that way. When Jesus came to the place, he looked up and saw him, and said to him, "Zacchaeus, hurry and come down, for today I must stay at your house." He hurried, came down, and received him joyfully. When they saw it, they all murmured, saying, "He has gone in to lodge with a man who is a sinner."

Mark 2:15–17

It happened, that he was reclining at the table in his house, and many tax collectors and sinners sat down with Jesus and his disciples, for there were many, and they followed him. The scribes and the Pharisees, when they saw that he was eating with the sinners and tax collectors, said to his disciples, "Why is it that he eats and drinks with tax collectors and sinners?" When Jesus heard it, he said to them, "Those who are healthy have no need for a physician, but those who are sick. I came not to call the righteous, but sinners to repentance."

Luke 22:8, 14, 17, 19–20

He sent Peter and John, saying, "Go and prepare the Passover for us, that we may eat." . . . When the hour had come, he sat down with the twelve apostles. . . . He received a cup, and when he had given thanks, he said, "Take this, and share it among yourselves. . . ." He took bread, and when he had given thanks, he broke it, and gave to them, saying, "This is my body which is given for you. Do this in memory of me." Likewise, he took the cup after supper, saying, "This cup is the new covenant in my blood, which is poured out for you."

John 14:27

Peace I leave with you. My peace I give to you; not as the world gives, give I to you. Don't let your heart be troubled, neither let it be fearful.

Mark 14:43, 46

Immediately, while he was still speaking, Judas, one of the twelve, came—and with him a multitude with swords and clubs, from the chief priests, the scribes, and the elders. . . . They laid their hands on him, and seized him.

Mark 15:16–20

The soldiers led him away within the court, which is the Praetorium, and they called together the whole cohort. They clothed him with purple, and weaving a crown of thorns, they put it on him. They began to salute him, "Hail, King of the Jews!" They struck his head with a reed, and spat on him, and bowing their knees, did homage to him. When they had mocked him, they took the purple off of him, and put his own garments on him. They led him out to crucify him.

John 19:25–27

But there were standing by the cross of Jesus his mother, and his mother's sister, Mary the wife of Clopas, and Mary Magdalene. Therefore when Jesus saw his mother, and the disciple whom he loved standing there, he said to his mother, "Woman, behold your son!" Then he said to the disciple, "Behold, your mother!" . . .

Mark 15:40–41

There were also women watching from afar, among whom were both Mary Magdalene, and Mary the mother of James the less and of Joses, and Salome; who, when he was in Galilee, followed him, and served him; and many other women who came up with him to Jerusalem.

Acts 5:12–14

By the hands of the apostles many signs and wonders were done among the people. They were all with one accord in Solomon's porch. None of the rest dared to join them, however the people honored them. More believers were added to the Lord, multitudes of both men and women.